10 Minute Money Makers

How to Easily Double Your Profits in Just 10 Minutes a Day

Jeanna Gabellini

"This book is right on the money! Jeanna delivers easy, fun and out-of-the-box strategies to dial in your inner and outer profit game. No matter how much business experience you have, this book will help you attract the kind of success that you've always wanted in a way that feels awesome!"

– Jack Canfield
Coauthor of *The Success Principles*™
and *Chicken Soup for the Entrepreneur's Soul*

*****

"If you have 10 minutes, you can have more money. I LOVE this book and these street-smart ideas! They are simple, fun, doable and take about as much time as it takes to drink coffee. Grab this book!"

– Dr. Joe Vitale
Author of *Attract Money Now* and star of *The Secret*

*****

"Do you want to massively increase your profits? Jeanna has broken down the process into bite-size chunks that are doable ... and she makes it super fun!"

– Robert G. Allen
Author of the New York Times bestsellers
Creating Wealth, Nothing Down, Multiple Streams of Income, One Minute Millionaire

CONTENTS

(W00T!)

woot woot/

exclamation informal

1. (esp. in electronic communication) used to express elation, enthusiasm, or triumph.

"I definitely get Fridays off, woot!"

DEDICATION

This book is dedicated to entrepreneurs who feel deep down in their hearts that they were born to be financially happy and know that it's not supposed to be hard.

Get out that Easy Button!

HISTORY

I was used to making six figures. I'd been christened with the Master Coach certification years prior. I was known as an expert on abundance. And I was flat-out broke. Paying-for-groceries-on-a-credit-card-that-had-reached-its-limit broke.

I was stressed, embarrassed and stuck. Fun times … *not!*

I tried for a year to get my money mojo back but I ended up in tears every week from the stress of not having enough money to pay my bills and watching the debt rack up.

My financial breakdown happened when my life was consumed with a proverbial romance-gone-bad and I wasn't giving my business any love. It only got worse when I searched high and low for a money breakthrough.

At some point, my new boyfriend decided he'd had enough of this broke coach stuff and suggested I get a job. A what?! You did not just tell me to leave my dream business to get a J-O-B, did you?

That was it. I snapped.

I used my anger to create momentum to break the desperation cycle. It was time to step back into my power and take intentional steps to get myself out of the financial hellhole I'd made for myself. Plus, I wanted to show my boyfriend that I was a sophisticated business owner who could get exactly what she wanted.
And I did.

Nine months later I had paid off every cent of debt,

tripled my profits and felt happier than I had in a long time. I had gone from less than $50,000 a year ... straight into six figures. I felt relief! My creativity, all by itself, started flowing again. Clients found me; I wasn't finding them. And it was *easy*.

My secret? **Baby steps!**

I took small steps on a daily basis that supported my goal of being debt free and getting my numbers back up to six figures. The way I saw it, I could either make this work or be depressed about failing at creating my dream business.

Thank goodness I made a comeback because it gave me good material for my first book, *Life Lessons for Mastering the Law of Attraction,* co-authored with Jack Canfield, Mark Victor Hansen and Eva Gregory. And my experience gave me compassion and appreciation for entrepreneurs who offer great value to their clients and customers but can't seem to make big increases in their income.

The other thing that made my financial comeback possible was being committed to the inner journey, and sticking with it no matter how long it took. Prior to that I'd been trying to get my business with strategies I'd developed out of a desperate mindset and needed any quick fix I could find.

Once I committed to long-term success I made choices that were inspired from a place of abundance and peace, not fear and neediness. If it took five years to get back in the money groove ... so be it!

But it didn't. In my wildest dreams I never thought I could turn things around so quickly. Appreciation became my daily focus. The more I appreciated what was working well in my business, the more stuff I created to appreciate.

I've since doubled my profits many times. A couple of times I did it from one month to the next. It felt miraculous to go from an average of $10,000 a month to over $20,000 and not from marketing anything. I vowed to sustain that increase and ignited a new business model.

Your turn!

********************************\=**

"In each moment you have a choice to decide what the outcome will be today, tomorrow, and the day after that. But once the day is past, it's your past life. You can bring it forward with you, or not."

*******************************\=**

THE SET UP TO WIN

This book is a godsend if you've been putting your heart and soul into making something happen in your business and you're still not rolling in the dough.

You need to see a spike in your profits fast, and the strategies I'm about to share with you are going to do just that (and make you do the happy dance, too)

Because all the marketing, branding, advertising, networking, coaching, hard work and long hours in the world will not make any substantial or sustainable difference in your bottom line until you:

- Shift **who** you are "being" in your business.

- Change **how** you think about your business.

- *Stop listening to everyone else*, and ...

- **Create your own profit-making system** that is fully aligned with *who you are, your inner knowing and natural way of getting things done.*

More effort, more work, more trying, more marketing, more networking ... *forget about it*!

You've already tried all of that. And it hasn't given you the kind of money and freedom you want.

It's time to take charge of getting money in the door with strategies that are actually fun (yes, fun!), simple and take less than 10 minutes a day to implement.

In fact, from this moment forward, if you're focused on

client or profit attraction and it feels hard ... STOP! That's an indicator that your timing is off, the strategy is not aligned with your values or you've got a belief that needs to shift before you move forward.

The right strategy in the ideal timing will seem like a miracle profit potion. It all stems from your inner game. If you don't pay attention to your mindset, the road to success will take detour after detour.

Everything I'm going to share with you here will get results. Massive results if you're enjoying the process. If one of the strategies doesn't turn you on, don't do it. It's that simple.

You've got to learn to tap into your own Inner Business Expert (aka Inner Guidance) and trust it more than any business guru. There's an overwhelming amount of information out there about growing your business and making money. I call them *suggestions*.

You need to be choosy about what goes into your profit plan. You want it to taste good before, during and after you implement.

Form your own opinion. Just because something made me six figures doesn't mean it's right for you. It's got to feel good to you. Seriously.

One of the main questions I ask my clients when we're strategizing for profit growth is ...

How does it feel?

If you're not thrilled about your business model or current profit strategies (as in, "HELL YES", I can't wait to implement this!) You may find your ideal solution by asking yourself these questions ...

- What is the ideal outcome I want from implementing this strategy?

- How can I tweak the strategy to make it ideal?

- What would make this over-the-top easy?

- Who can help me execute this with ease and professionalism?

- Am I making up a "story" based on past negative experiences or future fear of failure? What's the new story I want to create?

- How can I turn this into a game?

- How can I bring creativity and joy to this?

- Which strategy can I align with and still manifest the ideal outcome?

The wealth journey wasn't meant to be hard. It's a way for you to step into your most creative, powerful and spiritual self. If you're not grounded and confident, your business will never experience the results that you most desire.

By the way, you don't have to have prior experience with wealth to begin creating it. It's never too late. You're never too old. And you most definitely have what it takes.

Slow down. Pay attention to your Inner Business Expert and you'll be led to the ideal people, resources and strategies to attract more than enough to lead a lifestyle and business you love.

DON'T RUN WITH SCISSORS

Increasing your revenue or spendable income is a common desire. Hey, I'm right there with you. I want to invest more into my business, personal growth, learning technologies, home improvements, retirement funds, college funds for my boys, dream car and boat, not to mention clothes, vacations, dinners, gifts, and charities. I could keep going but you know what I'm talking about.

This book will help attract the profits you want and so much more. But heads up, there are a few things you want to avoid on this journey to doubling your money (otherwise it could be painful and unproductive!).

1. **Stop looking at your past reality unless you achieved financial abundance.** If you have, then look at what was different during that time. What were you mentally focused on? How did you treat your money? Were you doing something different  strategically? What do you think started your upward spiral?

2. **Don't beat yourself up about the current state of your financial affairs.** Logically, how does that help you? You can't get new ideas, solutions or more money when you're down on yourself, your business or someone else that you think caused this misfortune. Get your head into creating what you want, not what is.

3. **Get your attention off debt accumulation.** The majority of us have increased our debt during hard times.

While seeing it rise may emotionally trigger you, you must focus on *revenue accumulation*. Powerfully make a decision to eliminate debt, create a simple strategy to pay it off (even if you have to start with incredibly small steps), and then give all your energy to attracting prosperity. DO what you can, feel good about it and it will fall into place faster than you could've ever imagined.

4. **Let go of trying *hard* to figure out your miracle money solution.** It's hard to hunt down a solution if you feel powerless or stuck. Trust that your solution will come once you've declared that you have decided to kick some bootie in the revenue department.

When I was at my all-time lowest point with my income, I had no clue how I would dig myself out of the "mess" I'd created. I wasn't feeling creative. Debt was at an all-time high and I felt totally out of integrity. But once I decided to take the situation back into my control, little by little ideal solutions revealed themselves.

5. **Never sell your soul to create money.** Don't try to market something that you don't truly align with, just to get money in the door. Don't take an extra job you hate and force yourself to tolerate it. Don't lower your prices for services or goods out of desperation. These actions will get you no further ahead because you'll feel disempowered. Yes, you may need to take some extreme actions, but make sure your heart is fully behind them so that they yield the desired results.

FIVE PROFIT PRACTICES

When your main focus is on increasing profits and expanding the reach of your marketing, it's incredibly easy to be taken down a dozen rabbit holes each day. Remember, the strategies are only as good as the mindset behind them.

If you'll think less of implementing the 1001 profit ideas you have and give more time to following these five, simple practices, you'll find that you'll have less stress and more profits without efforting.

Your "monkey mind" will want to divert you, but don't give in. Profitable businesses use some version of the following practices and have incredible results.

1. **Always begin each brainstorming session, networking conversation or task, knowing exactly what you want to get out of it.** Never just show up and plunge into the task at hand without sitting down and giving conscious thought to your ideal outcome for each segment of your day.

2. **Tap into your Inner Business Expert several times each day.** Most people save their spiritual connection and intuition for after-work hours or when there is a crisis. When you decide to partner with your inner guidance, your business genius will be at full power. You can access out-of-the-box solutions, create new products and services, and feel at peace no matter how chaotic things might

appear.

3. **Ask yourself, "How can I make this more fun, easier and increase profitability?"** It's amazing what can happen when you ask yourself a powerful inquiry. It's even better when you use this question to make an already good thing even better. Go through all the main areas of your business at least once a month and use this inquiry. And don't forget to connect with your Inner Business Expert before you answer.

4. **Use the talent and expertise of others.** You may be brilliant at several things but there are other people who can put a different spin on what you're already doing and you can change your entire marketplace. When pondering your newest offering or tweaking a system, ask colleagues how they might improve what you're doing. It's best to use this practice before things go haywire. Join masterminds and get coached by people who freely share their information. Yes, you'll have to ask questions that expose your weaknesses, but you'll be rewarded handsomely.

5. **Stretch yourself.** It's easy to fall into a pattern of doing only what you need to get by. Challenge yourself every week to go beyond what's normal for you. If you never give services and products away, do it. If you give everything away, stop ... charge more. Use new technology to simplify the way you market or deliver your goods and services. Hire a coach that will cause you to think HUGE. Hire someone to help you market, file, or do customer care ... before you think you can afford it! Commit yourself fully to a project that scares the pants off you but has high rewards (because YOU CAN handle it!).

****

"Connection to your Inner Business Expert trumps ANY sales strategy."

****

MAKE MINE A DOUBLE!

I've always believed that people could achieve great things in little time, but it never seemed to happen to me. I thought that maybe I just wasn't old enough or smart enough. I read tons of books, attended seminars and taught cash flow workshops for years. But I couldn't seem to make big leaps in profit until I stopped trying so darn hard.

I doubled my income in one year. That taught me that it was possible. I did it a couple more times after that. Once I did it from one month to the next simply by releasing my attachment to which revenue source was going to be my big money maker that month.

What about you? Does it seem impossible to double or triple your income this year? What about this quarter?

The reality is that it can be done at any stage of your business, and in any time frame. How easy are you willing to let it be?

It takes the same amount of effort to create $100,000 as it does $10,000. Often it's actually easier to use a bigger number as your profit goal because it forces you to think smarter, be more creative and get outside of your normal (same ol', same ol') strategies.

One shift in mindset or one inspired strategy can be all it takes to see the evidence of this truth. Let your first step be to believe that doubling your profit isn't a big hairy deal. If you see doubling your money as too good to be true, you'll either not bother with creating a goal around it or you'll get incredibly attached to it.

If you see it as a normal occurrence, your negative emotions have nothing to grab onto. They won't stick. You'll be able to think clearer and make decisions based on what you want, not from fear.

My client, Tom, decided to do an impromptu marketing campaign. He told me he made $50,000 in a week. I asked, "What was your goal for the launch?" He said, "$50,000."

I told him next time go for $100,000. Why wouldn't you go bigger if you trust that you're going to get what you plan for?

There is no more energy you need to double what you make now (or massively increase it!). Plan bigger and usually you'll manifest bigger if you're tapped into your inner resources and confidently take inspired actions.

****

"The only reason you haven't doubled your profits in one year or less is that you haven't made the decision to do so and then jumped in with both feet."

****

DECISION TIME

You opened this book because you want an easier way to substantially increase your profits. The first step is to make a decision about what you really want in the next six months to a year. Forget five years from now, it's time to make some serious progress right here ... right now.

"Realistic" is not in my vocabulary. *"Realistic" is an excuse to lower your standards.*

Everything is possible when you make a "no kidding" decision to make some changes and then get your heart and soul behind it. Some crazy stuff will happen  when you move forward with confidence and eliminate failure as an option. The only thing you need to be cautious of is attachment to the end result.

Attachment is how you feel when you don't see results and you feel like you'll come unglued if they don't happen fast. Your happiness depends on the result. That feeling is a telltale sign that you're attached and disconnected from your power. Your inner peace is attached to having something happen vs. being okay where you are in this moment. It's directly connected to anxiety.

Not conducive to attracting abundance of any sort.

I've doubled and tripled my income from one year to the next several times. I've also done it from one month to the next and sustained it. Making a decision about what was going to happen next was the single most powerful thing I did to turn my life around.

Here's what you can do to get back into alignment with creating more than enough money.

1. **Draw a line in the sand**. Make a choice that from this moment forward you will attract more money and create a structure and habits that support a new and improved level of wealth. You have to mean it (even if you don't know how the hell you're going to do it at this moment). You need to be hungry for change.

2. **Believe.** You must *believe* you can do this. Even if you are scared that this time won't be different from all the other times you made this choice. You're going to take some actions that will not allow you to slip out the backdoor on yourself. Take a little bit of effort now to support your BIG goal.

3. **What is it *exactly*** that you want to be different? If you want more money to come in the door, how much and how often? Do you want an extra $10,000 this year or every month? Do you want your business to gross an extra million or net an extra million? When?

This month?

This year?

By next year's end?

You have to choose or it becomes one of those "someday" goals (aka a wish!).

If you choose an amount that feels way out of reach, then make it smaller. If the amount you have chosen feels too small and you'll still be wishing you had more money after it comes, then make it bigger.

Most importantly, whatever amount of money you are choosing to have, mean what you say. *This is so simple, but this is where most people fall down and the rest of their efforts don't yield successful results.*

And one more thing, *it's nobody else's business what numbers you choose.* Some people might judge your numbers as too small or big based on their own life. As long as you feel solid about your choice and you're not wimping out on yourself, go with it!

4. **How will you spend the money?** Again, this is your money and you need to be emotionally connected to it. Where is it going to go? If you are going to pay debt off, make a plan for how you will do it and then decide where the money will go once the debt is paid off.

Now you have the beginnings of a plan. That was easy, huh?! If you're going to save money, how much and where? You may have to do a little thinking and research to complete this step. If you want to expand your business with some of this extra cash, it may take you some extra planning, but you will be very excited. This excitement will help move you toward success.

5. **Clarify and write down how this is going to feel** once accomplished. I know to some of you this step will sound like a waste of your time. *Do not skip this step.* You want to make this goal so real in your mind and heart that you run, not walk, to more wealth.

6. **Create exact actions and habits** that you will implement, starting today, to support this goal of increased wealth. You may need to take only a few actions. This is not rocket science. For some of you, it may simply be a matter of creating accountability. You already know what to do. Yes, you may have to create an entirely new

relationship with money. You may need to set a date to quit your job or get rid of or add new team members.

Yes, you may dread a couple of things on your list, but will you be happy once you do it? If the answer is "yes", keep it on your list. Break down big actions into small steps so they're digestible. Consistency is paramount.

7. **Inspired action.** You may have heard this a million times but are you really practicing it? Are you taking actions that feel good? Are they someone else's "shoulds" or are they truly something you have chosen to do? Your intuition is talking to you. Are you listening?

8. **Who is going to support you?** Are you committed enough to see this goal through? Will you continue to trust that you will succeed, even when you don't think there are any signs of improvement over a long period of time? Who is going to assist you in a way that truly works for you? Bring in the big guns!

IN IT TO WIN IT!

If you really want to double the amount of money in your bank account and wallet, then implement the eight steps in the prior chapter in the next 24–48 hours. Calendar it. Get someone to watch your kids. Order health food to be delivered. Hole up in a comfy spot. This entire process may take as little as an hour or two. There's a huge return on your time investment. It's beyond worth it.

Some years ago I read *Adrift* by Steven Callahan, who was lost at sea in a small raft for seventy-six days. His boat had sunk west of the Canary Islands. He was able to write his book only because he was committed to getting back home and living. It wasn't a matter of "if" he got home, he always thought about what he was going to do "when" he got home.

Every action he took to keep himself alive was inspired from the passion he felt about getting home. He always found a way to eat, drink and keep his body working from his belief that he could survive at sea alone. And that he did!

How passionate are you about being wealthy? Get yourself into the same frame of mind as Steven. It's not a matter of *if* you will be more prosperous, but *when*. I vote on choosing it for you … **now**.

THE MAGIC OF
10 MINUTES A DAY

When I had my first son it was a huge wake-up call to think about a different business model. No longer could I work whenever I felt inspired because there were diapers to change, nursing, and connecting with my baby. Plus, it didn't help that I wasn't getting much sleep those first few years.

My mom stepped up to watch my first and second son part-time until the oldest began kindergarten. And I had to drastically change my mindset about how much time I needed to work to continue growing my business and be a good mom.

I still wish I had more time to work. I absolutely love the creativity that pours through me, and the accompanying personal growth, because I'm a business owner. And I have a boatload of evidence that profit creation takes only as long as you think it does. I work about 25–30 hours a week on average. I take a ton of 3- and 4-day weekends off as well as a couple of week-long vacations a year. Summertime Fridays are my water-ski days.

My intention is to continue streamlining and focusing on time abundance so I can work abroad with my family a month or two once a year.

Since time is a hot commodity in my life, I've had to rely on my inner game more and productivity less to increase my profits. And great news! I have some amazing strategies to generate record-breaking sales, not only in my business, but also in your business every year you implement them.

Now you can seriously double your profits and it will only take about 10 minutes a day!

You don't need to do the same strategy every day (unless it feels good). If you only have five minutes to devote to your profit attraction, at least take a small action step using the profit strategy of your choice.

Consistency is more important than the amount of time you spend doing it—quality over quantity.

Each step you take has a compounding effect (just like interest compounding from a solid investment portfolio).

Remember this riddle ...

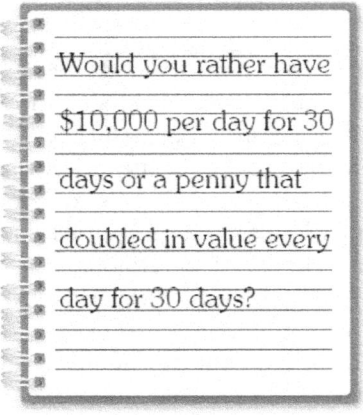

Would you rather have $10,000 per day for 30 days or a penny that doubled in value every day for 30 days?

Even though the *big* amount looks like a winner at first glance, the doubling penny will yield over $5 million at the end of 30 days. If you chose $10,000 per day you'd only have $300,000 at the end of 30 days.

Compounding interest is often called the eighth wonder of the world because it seems to possess magical powers, like turning a penny into $5 million. Taking baby steps daily to grow your business creates the same kind of magic on an energetic level.

Every time you take intentional steps to attract new income, your confidence grows. You feel proactive. You partner with your Inner Business Expert. The ideas flow more easily each day. And once you see some evidence that you're getting results, you attract more evidence.

The evidence will begin to multiply (the magic of compounding again!) and pretty soon you'll be debt free, savings accounts growing like a weed and more money in your bank account than you're used to having in your entire life.

Appreciate every shred of evidence. Feelings of joy. A client inquiry. A cool idea. Easily finding a business resource. Connecting with a new referral partner. A new sale (no matter how small!).

Any positive evidence indicates that you are making progress toward your desired results (sometimes long-awaited).

IMPORTANT: Once you take action, trust that what you've done has created momentum. Don't make the mistake of thinking it didn't work if you don't immediately have a waiting line around the corner with people who want to buy your stuff.

The compounding magic trick will surprise and delight you in a short amount of time, but don't wait around for it. Just keep taking those baby steps.

When I made the decision to somehow find a way to pay off my mountains of debt, I was in it for the long haul. I didn't care if it took me five years to handle it, I was going to continue following the debt elimination plan I created for myself.

At first the only thing that happened was I felt empowered because I was being proactive. I was proud that I had stopped whining about it and was doing something different.

About one month later I got my first big "win." I found just enough money to pay off my smallest loan. It was a small chunk in my debt mountain but, *wow!* It felt so good to know I'd have one less financial obligation each month. It got me very motivated to attract new profits so I could focus on paying off another obligation.

My profit strategy was very simple: Give five-star service to my current clients and anybody who inquired about my products and services.

I didn't know what else to do. I was fresh out of genius ideas. But I must tell you, I was committed to that focus of "lovin' 'em up". I appreciated my clients and let them know they were my priority. If even one of them stopped coaching with me at the time, it would've drastically impacted my resources.

Most business owners who need a cash infusion tend to give it their all and then stop as soon as their immediate money crisis is over. It creates a pattern of quick fixes with no consistent cash flow. Crisis, focus, cash, crisis, focus, cash ...

If you keep your eye on the end result and align your inspired actions with a well-thought-out plan, you can skip the crisis step in the pattern.

I'm not against strategizing for a quickie cash infusion. When you need one, you need one. But use it as a springboard to a profit breakthrough. Make a plan for changing the way you relate, attract and spend money after you get relief from your cash infusion.

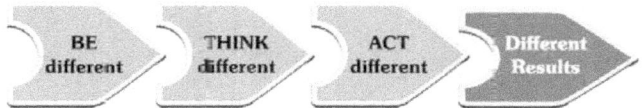

If you will devote 10 minutes a day to manifesting massive profits (and having a helluva lot more fun), I got your back on this one.

Choose whichever strategy inspires you each day or build on the step you took the day before. Baby steps create momentum. Momentum attracts kick-ass results. And it's a blast making money when you're not pressuring yourself to do stuff you don't like.

Be aware, you may find yourself putting off your 10 minutes of profit focus until the end of the day for various reasons. Do your best to do it at the beginning of the day. Here's why ...

- It will boost your confidence and mojo for the rest of the day.

- You won't rush through the activity.

- You'll have all day to come up with additional inspired profit ideas.

- Fires in your business, kids, and life won't get in the way and you won't have to put it off until tomorrow.

These 10 minutes are your key to creating a business you'll

love and that takes care of your financial desires. If you want your business to change, the 10 minutes are worth it. It's a new practice. Practice takes time.

PRACTICE ABUNDANCE

I'm a big fan of paying attention to your habits, both your habitual behaviors and thoughts. Some of your habits are intentional to live a smoother and happier life. However, some aren't even in your consciousness.

Most things you're miserable about in your life keep being generated by one or more of your patterns. A pattern is literally just a thought or action that you practice over and over.

After you practice something for a few weeks (or even a few days!) it becomes a dominant vibration. You attract more of the thoughts and actions you practice. Pretty quickly you have a new habit that you may not have intended. And in business, that can mean the difference between paying bills or losing your home.

For instance, I noticed Thursdays became days where I felt a lot of pressure. I usually don't work on Fridays so I would cram any leftover appointments or unfinished business onto my Thursday priority list. Then at day's end I'd feel disappointed that I didn't feel like I was complete with my work.

It was not a conscious decision. It just seemed to happen. This is how easy it is to get set with a behavior. I had to consciously create a new schedule for my Thursdays. Now I take no appointments after 11 a.m. and I block out at least three hours in the afternoon for special projects. Now I leave my office on Thursdays feeling productive, creative and relaxed!

It works the same way with attracting abundance.

You've probably heard that it takes 21 days of repeating an action or a thought before it becomes a habit, right?

- How many of your current habits do you think interfere with attracting more sales? Which ones work really well?

- Which habits suck up your time?

- Which business practices give you extreme joy? (Hint: these can lead to the best strategies to monetize your business!)

Take a moment right now to actually answer the questions above. If you don't, you probably have a habit of not taking time out to create powerful new habits.

Habits that support my abundance and peace of mind:

- Daily 20-minute walks to clear my head.

- Mastermind meetings.

- Weekly business meetings.

- Delegating work to my fabulous virtual assistants (VAs).

- Setting my intentions for each day (I do a maximum of 6. I use Stephen Covey's 6 Big Rocks formula).

- Scripting out goals (Writing stories about my goals, as if they'd already manifested).

- Tracking my income/expenses.

- Breathing purposefully.

- Going to the gym after work.

- Creating specific goals in all areas of my life.

- Having structures in my life that keep me accountable to my goals.

- Listening to uplifting CDs.

- Checking email only 3 times a day.

Habits I used to practice that created barriers to easy profit attraction:

- Checking email too many times a day.

- Reading almost every joke that got sent to me in email.

- Tearing articles/recipes out of magazines and then spending time to file them.

- Responding to everyone's request before I worked on my own projects that would grow my business.

- Being overwhelmed on a daily basis.

- Flying by the seat of my pants in the marketing department.

- Making business plans without accountability.

- Not forecasting with my finances.

- Being complacent about my team's performance.

- Not delegating enough.

- Worrying about not making my targets.

- Not being clear with my team about deadlines.

Your thoughts drive your decisions for your behaviors and actions. Practice a thought often enough and your behavior and actions will follow its lead. For instance, if you constantly worry about not having enough money, you'll create behaviors based on fear. You'll play smaller. You'll try to hang on to the money you have versus playing to win.

But if you decided that you were sick and tired of worrying about attracting enough money, you could intentionally practice empowering habits right now.

Your new habits can be big or small. Your frame of mind and personality will dictate what is best for you at this moment. I like to incorporate small and big habits when I want to increase my abundance. The small habits keep me grounded on a daily basis and are easy to accomplish, which gives me confidence.

The big habits create change quickly. They are defining. For instance, the last time I acquired more debt than I was comfortable with, I shredded all my credit cards except for my American Express business account. That was powerful for me because I showed myself that I was committed to the new goal and I took away my choice about creating new debt. This strategy isn't ideal for everyone, but at the time it served me well.

I also created spreadsheets that tracked my income and my balances of all debt. This was big for me to create, but a small thing to fill in every week.

Which practice are you willing to take on to step up your prosperity game? Once you've made a decision, clarify how you'll stick to practicing this new habit while you're in progress to it becoming natural for you.

By the way, all habits are *your* choice. Good, bad or ugly … you are the one who practices them. You can change them at any given moment. Do something different. Make it a game. Have some fun with the changes.

LET'S DO THIS!

****

"I believe in happy endings. They just take practice."

****

Profit Attraction Strategy #1

A "NO-KIDDING" DECISION

Let's get you warmed up with the easiest strategy of all. It'll take less than a minute, and unfortunately most business owners never do it. So do this and you'll be ahead of the crowd.

Decide "no-kidding" what your desired profit outcome will be for this week. Decide what you most want to sell. Decide it will be easy and that you know exactly what to do or be in order to have it happen.

A decision is concrete. It's a "yes" or a "no". What do you want most?

Everything you do from the moment you make your decision is based on your decision. You move forward with full expectation (but non-attachment) that you *will* get what you want. Period! The end!

Last year I decided to launch a new coaching program. At first I was very focused on the content I was going to deliver. But once it was all systems go, I thought about attracting about $40,000 to $50,000 from the program. But it wasn't a solid decision. I'd never made that much money from a 10-week program so I had a bit of fear. Could I really pull this off?

I hadn't yet stepped into my power and made a decision.

What I *really* wanted was to have my first six-figure launch. It pretty much felt like fantasy, not reality. I had no idea how to do a launch of that magnitude. But I kept thinking about how cool it'd be to actually pull that off and become better at marketing in the process. I love a good challenge so I used the launch as a structure to step up my game as a business owner.

I made a decision. I was going to have a six-figure launch. I called it my "Big Girl Launch" because I was going to have to fully step into this or it wouldn't work. I had no proof at all that this would be successful.

From that moment forward every brainstorming session with my team, every strategy I put in place, and every thought I had was about playing to win. And I was going to have a six-figure launch.

I did it. And it was probably the most fun I'd ever had in my business. Did my doubts creep in once in a while? Hell yes! I had told so many people what my goal was and I wanted to be able to tell a story about a launch with a happy ending.

I based every thought and action on the decision that this was a six-figure launch.

You play differently once a decision is made. No back doors. No worrying. NO attachment to it happening. I felt happy. I was going to go for it. And if it didn't happen, that was okay, but I wasn't focused on that option.

Business owners who dig the Law of Attraction talk a lot about intentions. I use that word a lot, too. But I truly think decisions are more powerful because you align everything you think, say, and do to back it up. It breeds confidence. And it shuts down your fears.

If you find yourself in a profit slump, make a decision about what's going to change. Sometimes you'll want to take lots of inspired action to make it happen and sometimes you won't need to.

I recently challenged one of my coaching groups to decide to manifest $5000 of new income within seven days. I told them to focus on their inner game more than strategy. I wanted them to experience the power of a decision and that outcomes aren't reliant on massive action.

After 72 hours someone had a check written to them for $5000. And she took no action to make it happen. Zero! It was a profound lesson for the group about the power behind a decision.

Your entire game changes when you make a decision. Not only do you think and act differently, but energetically your vibration increases. Synchronicities start popping up. Your senses become more acute. Creativity is ignited. You begin to feel more calm about money in general.

A powerful decision is like turning on your profit switch to *go*. So if you're griping, stressing or wondering how to make more money, make a decision to get some now. You don't even have to know "how" before you make the decision. As Nike says, "*Just do it!*"

So … What's your decision?

PROFIT ATTRACTION STRATEGY #2

FOLLOW UP

I used to think follow-up was something you were "supposed to do" after you got a lead at a networking group. (Cut me some slack, okay? When I first started my coaching business in 1996 I'd never been on the Internet and had to learn about email!)

Follow-up felt like a chore. Not anymore! I see it as easy money, baby.

Here are a few easy ways to follow up and create a deeper connection with your tribe, former clients and newbies and get effortless sales.

Check in with past clients.

I discovered this one by accident Whenever one of my former clients would pop in mind, I'd shoot them an email. It was a casual, "How are you? What are the three coolest things going on with you right now?"

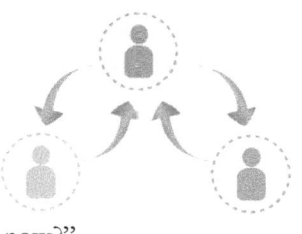

I had no agenda except to see how they were doing.

They'd give me updates and often would talk about an issue they were dealing with. I asked if I could help. Many of them booked a coaching session immediately. They just needed a little reminder that support was available.

Every time a customer purchases a product or service (or even downloads a free gift!) send a thank you email, card, small gift or a fun two-minute video.

If you can automate this process, even better! You want your customers to feel good before, during and after the purchase. And then follow up with one or more emails to check in on them, give them more value and make suggestions about other offers that they'd love and are congruent with the first purchase.

I once threw together an autoresponder email sequence (each email took less than 10 minutes to create!) for a bonus I gave away online. The email said to reply to me if they needed help and I'd hop on the phone with them for a 15-minute strategy session with no strings attached.

Over the last year, that autoresponder has made me thousands of dollars. People hop on the phone with me and receive great value. If I think they'd benefit by buying something else I offer, I tell them about it. No real sales pitch. I just share some options and then follow up our session with a recap by email with website links to the options I suggested.

Send customers a feedback form or a survey.

I do this after every program I facilitate. It anchors the value they received; you'll get awesome testimonials and great suggestions about how to improve your products, services, delivery systems and customer service.

Testimonials on your website can be the deciding factor for future customers to buy.

I once received a flyer in the mail for an audio cassette program (yes, back in the 90s). The quality of the flyer was horrific but they had dozens of amazing testimonials. I thought, "I want to feel the way these testimonials describe!" So, I picked up the phone and ordered it. This program was several hundred dollars and I still recommend it to my clients every month. It was *really* good.

Great testimonials can save really bad marketing and put some money in your pocket!

PROFIT ATTRACTION STRATEGY #3

OFFER PAST CLIENTS A DEAL

I appreciate anyone who has spent money with me. No matter how much money they spent, my goal is to give them extreme value. Happy buyers will be repeat customers. Make it easy for them to say "yes" with a special time-limited offer!

I bought a VIP package from one of my clients to help me be more time efficient (you never know where your next sale will come from! Be open to the infinite ways). She really made a big impact on how I organized my time and dealt with email.

During the holidays she sent out an email offer to past clients for a discount on coaching packages that included varying amounts of coaching hours. I immediately bought six hours and gifted half of them to my mom. BAM! I was an easy sale for her because I had already received huge value when I used her previously.

Be sure your offer . .

- Is compelling by clearly describing the benefits.

- Has irresistible pricing (make sure you show them the normal price and/or discount percentage).

- Has a limited time or quantity.

- Shows them how to purchase ... do they go to a special webpage, use a coupon code, call or walk in?

- Thank them for being your amazing customer or client.

- Isn't too wordy or confusing. The simpler, the better.

Beware: You may get more takers than you expected (a good problem to have). If your offer is a 1:1 service, book out plenty of time in your schedule. If it's a product, have all systems in place to deliver via email or mail with ease. You can simply discount something you already sell, or repackage it in innovative ways.

PROFIT ATTRACTION STRATEGY #4

A QUICKIE GET 'EM IN THE DOOR OFFER

This is a slightly different version of Profit Attraction Strategy #3. This strategy is for turning on a bunch of new people to what you have to offer.

The strategy is to make an offer that will give awesome value, won't take a lot of time for them to consume and is about $200 or less. You want there to be minimal friction to jumping on this offer.

Your offer can be anything you already sell, or bundle several of them together (don't be afraid to mix and match services and products).

If you offer a singular product or service, give a super steep discount. You want the offer to be irresistible. Remember, this is a way to get them in the door fast. Almost like paid advertising.

Once they get a taste of your stuff (and fall in love) you offer them something else that is congruent with what they just bought and get them farther down the road to their goal, solution or desire.

I used this strategy when I needed a fast cash infusion a few years back. I sent out three emails to my entire list for a 1:1 hour-long mastermind. In the email I gave several ideas of what they could accomplish during the mastermind. I painted a clear picture of some irresistible outcomes.

I offered the sessions for pennies on the dollar of my normal rate, which made it very easy for people to say YES! Both old and new customers jumped in. I was shocked by how well this strategy worked because it was so simple to put together.

The offer had a quantity limit—I only have so much time to do 1:1 sessions—and I made thousands of dollars doing my favorite thing: coaching.

At the end of the mastermind session I suggested specific products or programs that I thought would fit their individual needs. BAM! More sales. Not everyone jumped on the up-sell, but I made enough money to soothe my cash crunch.

Profit Attraction Strategy #5

JUST ASK

Why, oh, why, do so many entrepreneurs sit in their office thinking, "If it's to be, it's ALL up to me?"

Talk about pressure and stress!

It's quicker, smarter and easier when you ask helpful people to help you get clients. Everyone you know is a referral source; however, some are better than others at sending you ideal referrals who're ready to buy.

People love to serve other people if we make it easy for them. If you don't ask, the answer is always "no".

Who can you ask to ...

- Refer you 1:1 clients?

- Promote you on social media or to their ezine list?

- Interview you on their radio show or for their blog?

- Help you write great marketing copy?

- Include one of your products as a bonus when someone buys something from them?

When I look for promotion partners I ask them to introduce me to other ideal partners. I've never had someone say "no". And some of their partner referrals are still getting commission checks for all of the customers they've sent me!

I have several part-time contractors on my team, which means they rely on other part-time clients to make a living. Whenever they have an opening for a new client who do you think they tell first? Me!

If they're on my team, it means I think they're experts at their position and I'm HAPPY to refer them. I want them to thrive. Over the years I've referred them dozens of times, filling up their business. It is my pleasure.

One of my longtime clients and friend owns a movie production company. I recently asked her to make a documentary starring yours truly. Why not?! She loved the idea!

If you're used to giving all the time, it's time to balance it out with some asking and receiving.

****

"Ask and you shall be delighted and surprised."

****

PROFIT ATTRACTION
STRATEGY #6

POWWOW WITH YOUR HIGHER SELF

When you need money fast, it can make you do things that you normally wouldn't do. You complain to your nearest friend or call Mom for soothing. You may reach out in a panic to consult your team members and spouse, too. You may even leak your worries on social media.

Stop! There is a much better source for generating ideas and confidence, and clarifying your next steps to get more money in the door.

Have a powwow (a powerful meeting of the minds) with the very person you need most ... your ideal client. And not just *any* ideal client. You want to chat it up with the one that will buy your most profitable service or product package.

This is a conversation that happens virtually in your mind.

Most of the time, you'll be grateful to get any client to say, "yes", when it's money-crunch season. But when it's time for a big cash infusion, go for the gold.

What is the highest-priced ticket you offer? Or what is your most time-leveraged offer?

For me, my highest-priced service is 1:1 coaching. My highest time-leveraged offer is my Flashpoint membership program. When I feel anxious about my cash flow, I get clear on where I most want people to spend their money with me.

Both of these options can be long-term sources of income because there is no end date to the service if my clients are receiving value. You *might* focus on selling a lot of one product if you knew the up-sell conversion was almost guaranteed.

Once you're clear on what you most want to sell, push away from your desk. Imagine the ideal type of person who would say yes to that offer. I think about how excited they would be after they purchased. I tap into their joy.

It's now time to bring out the big guns. It's time for a chat ... higher self to higher self. Yep, a virtual conversation that happens in your mind where you connect to the heart space of your ideal client and have a conversation.

Usually when you really, Really, REALLY need to make more money you begin feeling that "pushing" or "forcing" energy pulsing through your veins. Once that switch is flipped, we put in extra effort and don't see results equal to our energy output.

This strategy forces you to step out of the "push" zone, step into your power and connect with your Inner Business Expert. Grab that Easy Button!

Your ideal clients want your solution as much as you want new business. You've come to seek answers directly from the source, from a place of curiosity.

Ask any questions that will lead you to things that you can do to empower yourself to manifest the ideal number of the ideal clients, lickety-split.

Here are some suggestions:

- What are your biggest obstacles to saying "yes" to my solutions?

- What do you need to hear from me in order to say, "yes"?

- What's the easiest way for you to hear my message?

- What do you see that I can shift to let you in?

- What's the best time to reach out?

- What should I do less or more of?

- Is there a product or service that I can tweak to be more appealing and valuable to you?

- How can I have more fun sharing my information with you?

- What would make you fall instantly in love with what I offer?

The answers will be short and sweet and will feel like *truth*.

Once the powwow is over, capture your ahas and ideas on paper. Decide which items will give you the most bang for your energy and go for it.

There is no greater advice on getting clients than from the

client himself. Yes, you may feel like you're just making up stuff in your head, but if it feels good, then you're raising your attractor-factor.

Your job is to trust the information you have received. You no longer have to try to convince your target market to buy, you'll be sharing from your higher self's perspective (from the heart).

You don't have to make dramatic changes to make the sale. If there is a next step you need to take, it will be obvious and it won't feel like you're efforting.

I have used this technique many times with corporate leaders with millions on the line, newbies just starting their business and veteran entrepreneurs who need a serious cash boost, and it has *never* failed.

You'll need to be relaxed in order to make that connection to your higher self. If you try to force clarity it won't come.

You can also use this technique to smooth out rumpled relationships with family, people you haven't seen in years and people you wish to attract into your life that you have yet to meet.

It may seem "out there" but try it. You'll become a believer.

PROFIT ATTRACTION
STRATEGY #7

RESOURCES RIGHT UNDER YOUR NOSE

Whether you work from home or in an office, it's easy to settle into your surroundings and create routines. Often you'll miss highly valuable resources under your nose that could help you create a new product or service, get a new referral or come up with a hot profit solution.

Think of an area of your business that you want to produce more money. The first step, as always, is to make a decision that you are going to achieve your desired outcome with this part of your business. You've got to be hungry for the goal and eager to be in the process of it unfolding.

Here are three resources that may give you immediate ideas, referrals, tools or support.

Resource #1: The Internet. You may use the Internet for Facebook, shopping, articles on your hobbies and YouTube for instructions on how to fix household appliances. But are you going there for info on how to accomplish your big fat juicy business goals? You can find inspiration and solutions to your marketing, website improvements and get new service and product ideas on a weekly basis.

Resource #2: Diversions. Have a lunch or dinner date with fabulous people you enjoy. Take vacations and walks. Go to the gym, go fishing, or go to an event. Watch a movie. Do anything you enjoy with the intention of letting in new information about your goal. The diversion is a diversion because it's not related to the goal. This allows your mind to "rest" from the goal and open up to new ideas, resources or cosmic connections.

Resource #3: A Mastermind Group. I'm a full-on believer in this as a huge resource!

What, you may be asking, is a mastermind? It is a group of people who meet to tap into the collective energy, support and knowledge to accomplish specific goals. A mastermind group helps you and your mastermind group members achieve success.

I was in the same mastermind with several coach friends for thirteen years and I got *huge* doses of ideas, specific business resources, honest and relative feedback on projects and ideas and extraordinary coaching.

I've been in paid masterminds that have given me access to business owners with much more savvy and wealth than I possess. And I'm in two additional masterminds right now that give me *at least* $100,000 worth of ideas, strategies and resources ... per year! Anytime I have a question about my next step, or want to tweak an idea, I ask the group and I get more than I ask for. I have entire binders full of their knowledge that I want to implement.

You already have access to what you need. Be willing to

play full out and enjoy the thrill of getting assistance!

PROFIT ATTRACTION STRATEGY #8

PUMP UP THE VALUE

I don't know about you but when I create a new product or program I put my all into it. Once I promote it and it's up on my website I have a tendency to just leave it there.

However, I changed my attitude when I saw several of my seven-figure colleagues dusting off their old products and pumping up the product value by adding some new material to it.

You know how Apple comes out with a new iPhone every year? I had to ditch my iPhone when I saw my man dictating his texts and got jealous. One new feature and I was on Amazon clicking the "buy" button!

Make your awesome product even more awesome and call it Version 2.0. Consider raising the price, but it's a good reason to revive and re-launch it.

All you have to do is come up with a new template, chapter, audio lesson or whatever and you've got your upgraded version. Do it yourself, delegate it to your team or hop on Fiverr.com (a website where people will do just about anything for five bucks).

Or add some group consulting or coaching to your

product and now you've turned it into a program! Add some email or Facebook group coaching in between sessions, too. You definitely want to increase the price if you'll be there in real time.

You can create your marketing campaign in 10-minute chunks. I like to play a game called *Write Marketing Emails in 10 Minutes or Less*. It's amazing how many times I win. It keeps you focused and doesn't allow time for your grumpy gremlins to come in and tell you that your copy sucks.

Profit Attraction Strategy #9

GET FAMOUS

As an entrepreneur you might not care about being famous. You just want to be paid like you are, right?

Getting famous can be easier than you may think. Media attention can get you hundreds of new fans. Plus, being mentioned in well-known publications or on television will boost your credibility rating.

Famous doesn't mean having your face splashed across the cover of tabloids. It means standing out in the crowd in your niche market to be seen as qualified, an expert or the ideal solution.

How do you get BIG attention when you feel like a small fish in a big ocean of your competitors?

Subscribe to HelpAReporter.com. Every day they send out requests from journalists who need sources for their stories on every topic under the sun. Thousands of journalists use this service.

Scope out popular bloggers who cater to your ideal

market and ask to be a guest blogger on their site. Give a free offer in your bio so you can capture leads and make future offers to them.

If you like to speak, there are hundreds of Google Hangouts and Telesummits on your topic. Often you'll be hobnobbing with experts more famous than you and they're sharing the event with their email lists. Another credibility boost is to share the stage with someone who is well-known in your industry. Again, offer a super high value bonus to capture names and emails.

Make a decision that you want media attention. I did this in 2004 and *The Wall Street Journal* called me. They were looking for a coach who worked with teens. That wasn't my specialty but I referred them to a friend, and told them if they ever wanted a resource for a story about business or team coaching, I was their gal.

Later that year I was quoted in large font in the career section in an article about corporate environments! *Easy!*

Like to talk? Radio show hosts are abundant thanks to iTunes and Internet radio shows. Find a show that will share your expertise with your ideal market and simply ask to be a guest. As a former radio show host I was grateful when I didn't have to hunt down new guests with hot topics. You can check out radioguestlist.com to get booked as a guest.

Get a testimonial from a celebrity. Send them your product free of charge or give them a taste of your services. Seriously. I gave my *Speed Dial the Universe* daily journal away to several of my industry's leaders and they've been posting on social media about it and ordering it as gifts for their V.I.P. clients. I wasn't looking for them to do that at all when I gifted the journal to them but it taught me a BIG lesson about freely sharing my hot products.

I did something similar last year when I let several high profile people have access to one of my programs. They loved it and endorsed it to their tribes. When someone promotes your stuff from firsthand experience it's very effective!

PROFIT ATTRACTION
STRATEGY #10

STEP INTO THE ELEVATOR

I built my coaching business through networking groups. I liked connecting with people but I always hated to say the little elevator speech to introduce myself at every meeting. I never perfected it and didn't try. I just said whatever rolled off my tongue in the moment.

I filled my coaching practice with 1:1 clients but I never was able to completely fill my tele-programs (seminars conducted over the phone). Two years ago something extraordinary happened by accident. I nailed my elevator speech.  I'll tell you how I did it in a few minutes.

Your elevator speech has the power to transform your business, even if you have an online business and never see people face-to-face.

How?

- It gets to the core of your message and trains you

how to speak directly to your ideal clients in a way that they fully understand.

- All of your marketing is based on your elevator speech.

- You can choose to post testimonials from your best clients to support what you say in your elevator speech to give it more oomph.

- It grounds you so that you can stand fully in your expertise. It's amazing how many people don't know how to clearly state what they do or what their product does. If it's not clear to you, how do you expect your market to understand it enough to buy?

I was able to figure out my elevator speech in less than 10 minutes during a powerful (and scary) exercise I did while attending a friend's networking workshop.

She told us to stand up and form two rows of people and face each other. She was going to give us less than a minute each to say what we offer to the person facing us. Then we were going to move on to the next person, and we'd have less time to get our point across with each new introduction until we only had 10 seconds.

I was forced to be succinct and think quickly on my toes. I immediately felt anxiety.

I took some deep breaths and asked myself what the most thrilling results were that my clients got from working with me. Their profits increased!

And I know that most people think they have to work harder and smarter to do that. But I don't teach that. What's unique about the way I coach is the emphasis on having fun and using attraction principles while doing what you love.

Yes, I teach *lots* of practical and proven business strategies. Yes, I do behavioral assessments, team coaching, corporate coaching and have lots of transformational products. But am I going to say all that?

No! If I rattle off everything I offer, my speech is just a data dump. Definitely not dynamic or worthy of questions.

So I went for the short 'n' sweet approach.

"Hi! I'm Jeanna Gabellini of Masterpeace Coaching Training. I help high achieving entrepreneurs and their teams to double (and even triple) their profits by leveraging attraction strategies, systems and fun."

People *smiled.* They wanted to know more. They either latched onto the part about doubling their profits or having more fun. It worked!

I noticed after that evening my copy for marketing felt stronger. I was more confident talking to potential clients and promotional partners because I knew exactly what to say. I had no idea that creating an elevator speech could be so easy or impact my business in such a positive way!

Would the experts in elevator speeches think my speech is awesome? I have no idea. But it rolls of my tongue easily because it's from my heart and I have the testimonials to prove it. In fact, I got a lot of the language from my clients' email raves.

The only reason coming up with a laser sentence or two about what you offer seems hard, is because you are either trying to get it perfect or packing in too much information.

In fact, you can use Profit Strategy #6 to help you get your creativity flowing.

PROFIT ATTRACTION STRATEGY #11

MONEY *FUNNEL*

Have you ever been told to create a marketing or money funnel? I'd heard about them but I never did it because I thought I would experience something similar to an ice cream headache ... instant brain freeze. Searing pain. Hard.

A money funnel is essentially your visual plan for how you will invite people into your tribe and then how they will move through your offerings (buy your stuff).

If you've created your money funnel but don't have a plan that moves people through it, kind of useless, right?

Your funnel begins at the top by naming the main ways that you get leads and visibility. This is where you turn them on. Curiosity is sparked and now they know you exist.

For instance, mine includes articles, speaking, and radio interviews.

Once they find you, the next layer of your funnel is to get

them to be a part of your tribe by giving them free and inexpensive ways to experience your stuff before they jump in with both feet.

I have audios, profit maps, daily manifesting journals, and visualization CDs.

The love affair has begun. Now it's time to get more intimate. You've kissed and gone to first base.

Next you name your low- (second base), mid- (third base) and high-priced offerings (home run).

When someone has experienced something in the $0–$25 price range from me, I'll introduce them to my more comprehensive learning products (low-end), coaching programs (mid- to high-end) and private coaching (highest-priced).

Each of my free bonuses and products has an automated email follow-up sequence that introduces my customers to the next step I want them to take with me.

When someone is in a program with me, there is another offer towards the end of it that introduces her (or him) to a way to get further support. Sometimes it's an up-sell (something more expensive) and other times it's a down-sell (something less expensive).

I like to give options depending on the program they just did and their budget. I'm not a hardcore sales person. I figure if they got value from their purchase and I share the next step from my heart, while clearly articulating the outcomes and benefits, I'm going to have a good amount of people continuing on with me.

And I love making the pricing irresistible to them and yet

still profitable for me. Win-win.

You may offer MANY things in your business but you must know your MAIN objectives. Where do you ultimately want to funnel people? What do you want to sell the most?

For instance, I sell seven products on my website. They are transformational products and have a ton of testimonials on their sales pages, but they are not my main objective.

I have two objectives in my business.

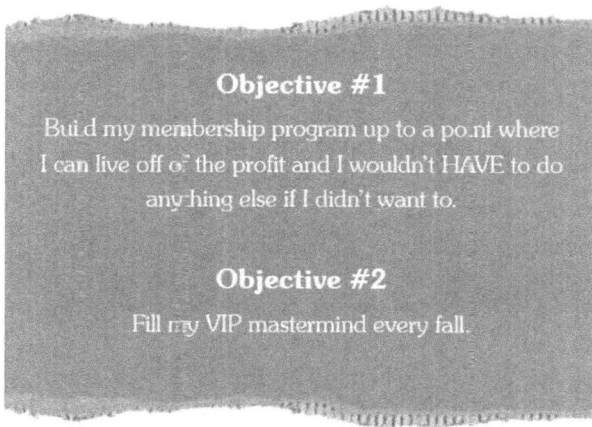

Objective #1

Build my membership program up to a point where I can live off of the profit and I wouldn't HAVE to do anything else if I didn't want to.

Objective #2

Fill my VIP mastermind every fall.

My membership program leverages my time and gives me the ability to serve a lot of people and make a great profit. It's an easy down-sell or cross-sell to ANYTHING else I offer.

My mastermind is time consuming because it also includes private coaching, but it gives me great joy.

Once you create your current *FUN*nel*, you'll want to map out how everything else you offer supports those objectives.

*If you're just starting your business you'll have to get creative and envision what you want your funnel to look like one to three years out. It will take time to actually create all of your offerings, so be patient and do them well.

It takes less than 10 minutes to create your *FUN*nel and about 30 to 60 minutes to figure out the up-sell, cross-sell and down-sell of each offer.

The first time I created my *FUN*nel I noticed an obvious gap. I had no way for customers to interact with me and get coached at a low price point. I felt like I was not being of service to some of the people who most wanted my support *and* I was leaving money on the table.

Within hours I came up with the idea of a membership program that was under $200 per month and gives extraordinary value. Two years later I still LOVE delivering the content and coaching the members in my Flashpoint program every month and it's a leveraged way to serve a lot of people without taking up a ton of my time.

Take 10 minutes right now to do your money funnel. Notice any gaps or offers that don't line up with your business plan, elevator speech and passion. You create a vacuum for profit attraction when these three things are aligned.

Your money FUNnel will be your guiding light to how you set up your behind-the-scenes marketing systems.

PROFIT ATTRACTION STRATEGY #12

THE PRICE IS RIGHT

Have you ever struggled with your pricing? What's too much? What's too little? What are my competitors charging? Should I go for lots of sales at a low price point or a higher price point with fewer clients?

What's your strategy for pricing?

Your emotions and limiting beliefs often dictate how you choose to price your products and services. Whether you feel you're charging too much or too little, it impacts your bottom line.

Even if they feel great, if they're not going to make enough profit, you'll either have to change the price or the way you plan to deliver your offer.

If you can't get yourself fully aligned with a price point, it won't work. If you're resistant even a teeny tiny bit, it's not going to work.

It doesn't matter who you're selling to or the product or service. If you charge what you really want and feel confident about, it makes for an easier sale.

Why? If you feel that you're charging too much, you defend the pricing or feel shy saying it. If the price is too little you resent the effort you put into your offerings and don't feel well compensated. Low pricing also has a tendency to have you under-deliver because there is no motivation if you're not being compensated well.

Your product or service doesn't even need to be the best or most brilliant out there. You just need to genuinely believe in the offering, know your own self-worth and ask a price that is satisfying to you. If you clearly spell out the value of your offer, your customers will see it as a great deal no matter how high it is.

What you think is a high price may seem like a bargain to someone else. And what you think is dirt cheap may be way outside of someone else's budget.

There will always be people who can't muster up the faith to make a decision to buy from you no matter how low your price. Other folks will get very creative to find a way to make it happen. You can't serve everyone, and you've got to make peace with that.

Benefits of raising your prices:

- You won't resent your clients.

- You will *want* to give them even more value.

- It increases your confidence level.

- You will make more profit and be able to hire other

people to do the things in your business that are not your strengths, or that you don't have time to do.

- You'll experience more joy because you'll be more aligned with your true vision.

There is also great value in charging what you feel is good right now, while moving your way into the bigger vision as your business and confidence grows. You can begin with a small step.

Your pricing needs to feel good, but not be driven by fear of losing clients. It also needs to be high enough that you are not only covering your overhead but making enough so that you're able to live comfortably. You also want to make enough money to invest back into growing your business.

When I first began my business, my first client received four coaching sessions a month and she paid me a whopping fifty dollars.

I poured my heart and soul into the coaching and decided to charge my second client one hundred dollars a month. At the time, it felt good and I was happy to have clients with whom I could practice my new coaching skills.

But fast-forward a year down the road. One hundred dollars didn't feel very good. I began raising my prices little by little until it was $350 per month for one-on-one coaching. I felt great about this price. However, my practice was beginning to be rather crowded. I felt like there were too many clients, not enough time and certainly not enough money for the amount of hours I was putting in.

My mind wandered to a vision I had a few years before:

Ten clients, each paying me $1000 per month to have me on retainer. *That* felt wonderful. I raised my prices again and changed the structure of the coaching. I was happy, happy, *happy* with this model for over a decade!

I saw less experienced coaches charging more than double what I was charging. I didn't care. My model felt great. I even paid a coach with less experience than me to coach me at $1800 a month. Even though the investment was a stretch at the time, I was getting great value and was committed to making it work.

Later, as I began to shift my business model again, I raised the prices on some services and lowered the prices on other services and products. The change felt very congruent with my overall strategy and felt great.

Any time I've ever charged a price that felt like too little or too much, it was an indicator of impending doom. The product or service didn't generate profit and I even lost money on some of them.

Being strategic about pricing is smart. How you feel will trump strategy in the end. Choose prices that more than cover your expenses, inspire you and make you want to shout from the rooftops about how much value your product or service delivers!

Do a quick inventory of your prices. Are they set up for making profit? How do they feel?

I know it may be scary, but change at least one price to be aligned with making profit and make sure it feels good.

Tip: I make it easier for my clients to have access to some of my higher-priced offerings by having a payment plan option.

******><***************************

"Choose prices that more than cover your expenses, inspire you and make you want to shout from the rooftops about how much value your product or service delivers!"

******><***************************

Profit Attraction Strategy #13

PREPARE FOR YOUR WINDFALL

Are you prepared for your business to grow as fast as you'd like?

Preparing for a massive increase is powerful because you're giving your goal energy, which creates a magnetic pull between you and the goal. If you create a plan now, before the windfall comes, it's much easier to make empowering money management decisions rather than spontaneous spending or investing based purely on emotion once the money comes.

I know a person who was interviewed on Oprah who wasn't able to leverage his publicity from the show. He didn't have enough of his books that he was promoting to keep up with the sales demand generated from his guest appearance.

Preparing for your windfall of success means you have to visualize what you want your business and life to be like as a result of having more money than is normal for you. If your goal is to double your income in the next six months, imagine having the money pouring into your bank account.

How will you spend it? Have you created a spending plan?

- Do additional savings accounts need to be opened?

- What new tax strategies will you need to put in place?

- Who will help you sustain increased profit growth?

- Does your website or brand need a makeover? Do you know who will do the work and what you want it to look like?

- Do you have systems in place to handle the new volume of business?

- Do you plan on vacationing? Do you know where, with whom and when? Do you need to make arrangements for your home, pets and business when you leave?

Count on doubling your profits and plan for it. Make decisions now based on your future success. Decide that the planning will be as exciting as the actual manifestation of money and so shall it be.

****

"Act as if it is so, and so shall it be."

*******×*************************

PROFIT ATTRACTION STRATEGY #14

THE DOUBLE IT GAME

Why start a business if it's not going to be enjoyable and support an awesome lifestyle? Exactly! Doesn't make sense, right?!

What is one of the best ways to have fun in your business? Make it a game with rules that you make up to suit your behavioral style.

Start with a game objective like ...

- Double your profits in two quarters.

- Double your contact list size in two months.

- Double the sales of your least expensive (or most expensive) product in 30 days.

- Double your referral partners in six months.

The objective needs to be something you can get excited about and that will nudge you out of your comfort zone in order to "win." The game needs to be

designed to inspire, help you master a skill and create new profits practices.

Create guidelines to help you win and have fun like ...

- Reach out to 1 new referral partner each day.

- Spend 2 minutes each morning envisioning celebrating that you won your Double It game.

- List 5 things that you appreciate about your business each day.

- Get 5 people to say, *"no"* to you each day. This is the game I played to fill my 1:1 coaching practice when I first opened my business. This practice takes away your resistance to hearing *"no"* and will have you reach out to more people. Pretty soon, you'll double the amount of *yes*es you get!

- Log at least 5 pieces of evidence daily that you're aligned with making more money.

- Set aside 10 minutes a day to focus on your Double It objective.

- Spend 10 minutes daily on social media to create value for your tribe and give them a call to action that supports your desired outcome.

If your game seems like a chore, you need to change it. Or get a buddy to play his own game, and check in with each other daily by text, email or voicemail. Make the check-in focused on your "wins" for the day or evidence that you will nail your outcome.

Focus on the progress you make, no matter how small. Games are meant to be played over and over so that you increase your skill level and have a good time doing it.

The first time I did a major marketing launch I made it a game. I focused on making goals that forced me to shift my fears into focus. I was scared to death to reach out to my peers and ask for their support. I didn't want to "bug" them.

I chose to make one of my main objectives to get 100 promotional partners and make it into a game. I began to have so much fun creating wild strategies to get *yes*es that swung to the other side of the pendulum. I began to ask anyone and everyone that I thought was a good match.

My other objective was to make six figures without stressing out. One of my guidelines was I could not use a marketing strategy if it felt stressful or time-consuming.

It was the most fun I ever had creating six figures. Play to win and add fun as a main component. How much fun are you willing to have in your game?

****

"Taking things seriously is seriously overrated."

****

DOUBLE YOUR MONEY VIBE

It's easy to get caught up in looking for miracle strategies to make money fast. "If you do X in your business, you can make millions," is the message coming from all directions. If you sign up for this class or that eCourse, you can make six figures in two weeks.

While certain strategies, investment opportunities and niches do produce results, it's all about how you resonate with that particular thing that makes it successful or not. Your emotions produce vibration and that is what controls your profits rising or falling. Your money vibe is what makes you collide with good deals, fast sales and all around good luck.

Except it's not luck. It's planned.

Intentionally changing your relationship with money has everything to do with how you relate to it This in turn creates a high frequency when you think about money and literally draws it to you like a magnet. Magnetizing money is in fact what is happening.

All you have to do to change your money vibe is make a decision today that you will relate to money with excitement. Begin making decisions like a six- or seven-figure CEO would. Act like you know what you are doing. Act like someone who  earns lots of money, is used to it, and has fun at money creation.

How do you do this if you've been consistently struggling with money? Let go of the reins. Quit whining, complaining, feeling victimized, trying too hard and all that crappy stuff you do when it comes to money. And quit being cheap, when it would serve you better to invest in quality. Stop saying you can't afford things ... because you are creating a self-fulfilling prophecy.

When you see something you want, decide you will have it, even if you don't have the means in this moment. Whenever you decide you want something, I mean *really* decide, you will find the means to do it. And it won't be from raiding the piggy bank. Although it could be. It's your choice.

The other sure fire way to raise your money vibe is to raise your vibe in general. Do stuff that is fun and reminds you that life is an adventure to be enjoyed. Whenever I go to my family's vacation home, I come home to several new sales. Going to the movies, reading good books, connecting with friends and gardening are great, too.

Doubling your profits from one month or year to the next is an inner journey. Pay attention to your Inner Business Expert, on a daily basis, so that your profit strategies align with your soul, making them highly attractive to your ideal customers.

Every business owner has the ability to source creative business strategies that can make doubling your profits happen faster than you could've ever thought possible.

I recently wrote a 30-second script to attract promotional partners for a coaching program I was launching. I paid $10 to have someone to read and record my script doing his best Barack Obama impersonation. I then sent the audio recording along with a short email message to dozens of my ideal promotional partners. I got more *yes*es because of that audio recording than anything I'd done prior.

It was easy, inexpensive, fun (I laugh every time I listen to it!) and got mind-blowing results. All I had to do was tap into my Inner Business Expert for a little creativity.

You have what it takes to double your profits this year. Tap into all of the resources readily available to help you do it. Invest in mentors and experts to help make your ideal profit path easier to follow. Have fun and allow it to be more fun than you ever imagined.

When life gets in the way of your profit goals, use that as fuel to rise to the occasion (after you give yourself permission to have a quick meltdown).

Right smack dab in the middle of writing this book, I found out I had to have surgery to remove a tumor (benign) in the palm of my right hand. I'm right-handed so I was bit miffed when I came out of surgery with a plaster cast on my arm that prevented me from writing or typing for a couple of weeks (not to mention not being able to cook, tie my shoes, lift up my kids or shower).

I went into "poor me" mode until some guy said, "Your tumor was benign, right?"

I stopped whining and I stepped back into appreciation that all I had to do was adjust my life for a few months. I would be healthy.

I decided that I'd find the time and inspiration to make my publishing deadline. This one-handed typing wonder finished two weeks ahead of schedule, which seemed totally impossible before I made the decision that all would be well.

Be open to receiving success without struggle or overwhelm. And when it becomes a bit hard, take a step back. Find a way to come back to your center and connect with your Inner Business Expert.

Trust your guidance because if you can't trust yourself, who can you trust?

Cheers to doubling your profits!

Jeanna ♡

FREE GIFT: MAP TO DOUBLE YOUR PROFITS

Download a FREE visual map of how I tripled my income in less than a year with ease and FUN! You'll also get your own visual map to fill in with your most important *Hell Yeses* for this year. **If it's not a "HELL YES", it doesn't go on your map.** This will make your next profitable steps *very* clear.

Grab your FREE Map to Profits by going to:

www.MapToProfits.com

For an abundance of resources to help you attract a business that provides more than enough money and joy, go to:

www.MasterPeaceCoaching.com

APPRECIATION

If I had clients who sucked my energy dry, my work would suck. Fortunately, I consider my clients, customers and tribe inspiring, brilliant, fascinating and some of the kindest people I have ever met. I consider my time in my office or at the computer pure joy. Really.

Some years ago one of the nicest guys in my industry, Jack Canfield, offered to publish my BFF Eva Gregory and me, and proved that writing a book could be done in a short period of time.

I never thought I'd write a second book but Rob Goyette, my marketing genius, suggested I do it. And since he's never steered me wrong, I said, "What the hell! I have no time to write it so we better find a fun and easy way to make it happen." And we did. Thank you, Rob, for inspiring me to have more fun in my business than I ever imagined (and the profits are sweet, too!).

And no business can survive without peers who are out in the forefront paving the way. Christian Mickelsen and my fellow masterminders have inspired, coached and supported me through some major growth spurts. Their votes led to the name of this book.

My team is made up of many special people who play their positions well. I couldn't have doubled it without them. Lauray, Amber, Don, Rob, Kaylyn, Sarah, Nancy, Susan and Victoria, *I freaking love you!* You can never leave, okay?

I also give daily appreciation to my family, friends (especially Eva, Wendy and Bridget), babysitters, housecleaners and everyone who helps me stay sane. It takes a village and I manifested the best!

BONUS PROFIT STRATEGY

Go on rampages of appreciation as often as possible. Keep a daily journal or tell a friend. And always tell your tribe and team what they mean to you. Appreciation is one of the easiest ways to shift your energy and get those profits pumping!